PAW-LAL'

PAW-LAL'

Prayers that bring supernatural breakthrough.

Pastor Murthlene Sampson

Copyright © 2018 by Pastor Murthlene Sampson.

Library of Congress Control Number:		2018912066
ISBN:	Hardcover	978-1-9845-5802-2
	Softcover	978-1-9845-5801-5
	eBook	978-1-9845-5800-8

All rights reserved. No part of this book may be reproduced or transmitted in any form or by any means, electronic or mechanical, including photocopying, recording, or by any information storage and retrieval system, without permission in writing from the copyright owner.

The views expressed in this work are solely those of the author and do not necessarily reflect the views of the publisher, and the publisher hereby disclaims any responsibility for them.

Scripture quotations marked AMP are from The Amplified Bible, Old Testament copyright © 1965, 1987 by the Zondervan Corporation. The Amplified Bible, New Testament copyright © 1954, 1958, 1987 by The Lockman Foundation. Used by permission. All rights reserved.

Any people depicted in stock imagery provided by Getty Images are models, and such images are being used for illustrative purposes only. Certain stock imagery © Getty Images.

Print information available on the last page.

Rev. date: 10/08/2018

To order additional copies of this book, contact:
Xlibris
1-888-795-4274
www.Xlibris.com
Orders@Xlibris.com
786456

Contents

Prelude ix

Part I
Destroy The Plot Of Satan

Chapter 1   Praying Against Spiritual Attacks 1

Part-II
Activate Your Blessings

Chapter 2   Prayers That Introduce the Blessings of God 13

Part III
Prophetic Prayers

Chapter 3   Prayers That Brings Wealth 25
Chapter 4   I Am Healed 37
Chapter 5   Take Spiritual Authority 49
Chapter 6   Supernatural Breakthrough 57

Part IV
Walk In Your Freedom

Chapter 7   As for Me And My House 71

"...Whatever you ask for in prayer—believe that you have received it and it will be yours."
Mark 11:24 (The Passion Translation)

Prelude

This book *PAW-LAL'* includes prayers that introduce God's miracles, healing, blessings, and supernatural release. A daily dose of prayer activates God's purpose for our lives. Once prayer becomes a discipline, we will see a great move of God that will introduce us to experience the supernatural realm. Prayer will put things in place and cause Heaven's response to what is declared on earth. Paw-lal', means pray, and the word *"Pray"* denotes an individual petition or request. Prayer is a verb and a verb require action. So, if there is an action then, there must be a re-action. When you act on what you need through prayers, God will acknowledge your inquiries.

Ten thousand dollars supernaturally went into my bank account with no trace, as to where it came or who sent it. I was never told by the bank that I had to return this money. God put it in my account, it's mine. Prayer can do this. Although God moves instantaneously, sometimes it happens within hours, days and even weeks. I have heard the cry of many people who desire to see a move of God in their lives. I have met others who have questions about why things are not happening when they pray. I have also heard people say, *"I have prayed, but I get no answers." "I have prayed so long, and hard, but there are no results." "Why isn't God answering my prayers?" "How long must I wait?" or "Am I praying the wrong way?"*

These questions are valuable and bring significant concerns as to why some prayers are not answered. This is what I have learned about why God doesn't answer prayers. Sometimes, God does not give us what we want, but He will always give us what we need. Unanswered prayers sometimes can be, because of the motives behind our prayers. If our desires or impulses are driving our prayers; God will take His time in answering. *James 4: ³ And if you ask, you won't receive it for you're asking with corrupt motives, seeking only to fulfill your selfish desires. (The Passion Translation TPT)*. Nevertheless, when we pray believing God's Word, and do it in the name of Jesus, we will receive exactly what we pray for. *"You haven't tried this before, but begin now. Ask, using my name, and you will receive, and your cup of joy will overflow." (John 16:24 Living Bible)*

Prayer can be one of the most challenging things to do, and many individuals have a hard time praying. Some people have prayed with no immediate results, which led to frustration, bitterness and even became angry with God. But we must *"pray without ceasing." (1 Thessalonians 5:18)*. This book will show you how to obtain answers according to God's Word.

Many of these prayers were written while I prepared for various sermons. While some were written during a season when the Leviathan spirit and the enemy had attacked the church I pastored and during a time of prayer shut-in, fasting and intercession. These prayers emanated from my spirit. The attacks caused many things to be delayed and hindered. But God continuously birthed great prayers in my spirit. I occupied every moment of my time in the Word of God and continually allowed Him to teach me. He imparted insight, illumination, and knowledge. There were great financial miracles that took place in my life and the lives of the saints. The plan of Satan was dismantled, while God's purposes overtook every area of my life and the life of His people. Jesus said to his disciples "...*when ye pray, believe that ye receive them, and ye shall have them" Mark 11:24*. These prayers will help you to connect to heaven to bring change on earth. Heaven will only deliver what we command it to perform.

When we pray what the Word says about God's promises for us, it will give us confidence and assurance that our prayers will not be in vain. Daniel prayed based on the promise that God made towards Israel in *Daniel 9:2-4 ² In the first year of his reign I Daniel understood by books the number of the years, whereof the word of the Lord came to Jeremiah the prophet, that he would accomplish seventy years in the desolations of Jerusalem.³ And I set my face unto the Lord God, to seek by prayer and supplications, with fasting, and sackcloth, and ashes:⁴ And I prayed unto the Lord my God, and made my confession, and said, O Lord, the great and dreadful God, keeping the covenant and mercy to them that love him, and to them that keep his commandments;*

When we pray based on the promises of God, we will obtain all HIS promises for our lives. One of the saints came into the office and showed me her checking account, with a balance of $40,000.00. She said, "I believed the prayer, and God did it." This saint had been waiting on God for over five years to fix a legal case, but when she prayed one of these prayers *"God responded."* Most of these prayers were written over a period of one year and were given to the saints to pray daily; this resulted in answers to prayers. Now it's your time to experience the same miracles and more of God's intervention through these prayers.

I have used some of these prayers on various occasions. I have a prayer line every Thursday, and miracles, upon miracles have taken place. Some of these prayers were used on the prayer line, and the results have been amazing. A woman was experiencing foreclosure and two days after the prayers; she received a letter from the bank stating that she can keep her home. Then, there was a woman who was stricken with cancer in her breast, and God healed her. The following week, she took a mammogram and one week after, the result showed that there was no cancer in her breast. There was a mother who was believing for her son to get off drugs. Two weeks after prayers went out, her son was completely delivered from drugs, after ten years of addiction. I have prayed for a woman whose husband, left her for another woman. She also, believed God after she prayed one of these prayers, and within six months, her husband left the other woman and returned home to her and the children. As you pray, expect to see God work a change in your situation. Let your faith be encouraged. Let your miracle begin NOW! As you pray these prayers, believe that you will receive.

Lift Your Faith and Let God do it now. It is time to arise and possess your inheritance.

Part I
Destroy The Plot Of Satan

Lest Satan should get an advantage of us: for we are not ignorant of his devices.

----- *2-Corinthians 2:11*

Chapter 1
Praying Against Spiritual Attacks

DAY 1

Job 41:1-10 Canst thou draw out leviathan with an hook? or his tongue with a cord which thou lettest down?² Canst thou put an hook into his nose? or bore his jaw through with a thorn?³ Will he make many supplications unto thee? will he speak soft words unto thee?⁴ Will he make a covenant with thee? wilt thou take him for a servant for ever?⁵ Wilt thou play with him as with a bird? or wilt thou bind him for thy maidens?⁶ Shall the companions make a banquet of him? shall they part him among the merchants?⁷ Canst thou fill his skin with barbed irons? or his head with fish spears?⁸ Lay thine hand upon him, remember the battle, do no more.⁹ Behold, the hope of him is in vain: shall not one be cast down even at the sight of him?¹⁰ None is so fierce that dare stir him up: who then is able to stand before me?

DISMANTLING THE LEVIATHAN SPIRIT

Today by the blood of Jesus
I send forth an apostolic anointing warrant
against every attack of the enemy.
I cancel every attack in the name of Jesus.
Every gathering of witchcraft spirit formed against
my ministry, my marriage, and my children, I call
them undone by the power of the Holy Spirit.

Every wickedness reinforced against my finances
and ministry, I disarm it in Jesus name.
Every demon assigned to frustrate my success
before its breakthrough, I tell it to get out!
I paralyze every attempt or attack of Satan against
my life and the generation to come.

Every decision spoken against me is null and void.
I break the power of demonic spells against my
money, career, business, and ministry.
I break demonic covenants and denounce all generational
spirits assigned to attack the growth and development of my
wealth, healing, prosperity, ministry growth, and miracles.
I declare all these things to be so in the
mighty and powerful name of Jesus,
Amen and amen.

....

Prayer of Declaration

Jesus, today I declare that I am free from every Leviathan spirit over my life.

....

DAY 2

Judges 6:1-6 And the children of Israel did evil in the sight of the Lord: and the Lord delivered them into the hand of Midian seven years. [2] And the hand of Midian prevailed against Israel: and because of the Midianites the children of Israel made them the dens which are in the mountains, and caves, and strong holds. [3] And so it was, when Israel had sown, that the Midianites came up, and the Amalekites, and the children of the east, even they came up against them; [4] And they encamped against them, and destroyed the increase of the earth, till thou come unto Gaza, and left no sustenance for Israel, neither sheep, nor ox, nor ass. [5] For they came up with their cattle and their tents, and they came as grasshoppers for multitude; for both they and their camels were without number: and they entered into the land to destroy it. [6] And Israel was greatly impoverished because of the Midianites; and the children of Israel cried unto the Lord.

DESTROYING FINANCIAL DEMONS

Today I bind every evil spirit and spell
that are attacking my finances.

I cancel every plan, curse, and economic
highjack against my finances.
I disrupt every dark force that is overshadowing my blessings.
I burn down every evil altar that exalts itself over my
finances and call forth the army of the Lord to Stop the
wicked devices that the enemy uses to bring poverty.
Every evil sacrifice working against my finances is canceled.
Every satanic curse is canceled.

Everything that was stolen from me let it be returned now.
Every evil stronghold that comes to my dreams,
I dismantle it in the name of Jesus.
Every unseen arrow that has been fired against my
finances is broken and rendered ineffective.
Let the fire that Elijah called down from
heaven, fall on every financial curse.
Every power that hates my financial wealth is now undone.

Every demonic stigma that is holding back my
portion, in the IRS, banking institutions, or previous
jobs, I command it to be released NOW!
I recover all my wealth and finances NOW!
I command every financial disruption into the abyss.
Let the Lord surround my finances with the fire of the Holy Spirit.

I call God's wealth upon my life now.
I release the power of the Holy Spirit upon my finances and
command all my finances, which are held up, to find me NOW!
I command all my God given resources to come to me now.

Let God arise, and my enemies be scattered.
In the name of Jesus, Amen.

....

Prayer of Declaration
Jesus, today I declare that every demon affecting my finances is destroyed.

....

DAY 3

2 Samuel 21:15-21 *[15] Moreover the Philistines had yet war again with Israel; and David went down, and his servants with him, and fought against the Philistines: and David waxed faint. [16] And Ishbibenob, which was of the sons of the giant, the weight of whose spear weighed three hundred shekels of brass in weight, he being girded with a new sword, thought to have slain David. [17] But Abishai the son of Zeruiah succoured him, and smote the Philistine, and killed him. Then the men of David sware unto him, saying, Thou shalt go no more out with us to battle, that thou quench not the light of Israel. [18] And it came to pass after this, that there was again a battle with the Philistines at Gob: then Sibbechai the Hushathite slew Saph, which was of the sons of the giant. [19] And there was again a battle in Gob with the Philistines, where Elhanan the son of Jaareoregim, a Bethlehemite, slew the brother of Goliath the Gittite, the staff of whose spear was like a weaver's beam. [20] And there was yet a battle in Gath, where was a man of great stature, that had on every hand six fingers, and on every foot six toes, four and twenty in number; and he also was born to the giant.*[21] *And when he defied Israel, Jonathan the son of Shimeah the brother of David slew him.*[22] *These four were born to the giant in Gath, and fell by the hand of David, and by the hand of his servants.*

DESTROYING GOLIATH DEMONS

Lord Jesus today
I revoke every satanic decree against my progress.
I bind every spirit that is trying to prolong my stay in the wilderness and declare that its power is broken NOW!
Every Red Sea confronting my promise be dried up.
Every Jericho wall that is blocking my progress, fall NOW!
Every Lot spirit trying to block my destiny moves away.
Every Lazarus trying to hinder my destiny,
hear God's Word now, and come to life.

Every Pharaoh that is hindering my next move is removed NOW!
Today I raise the standard of God and
cause the enemy to be scattered.
Every confident spirit against my destiny has lost its battle.
Today you are given notice that it's over. I
command you to go in Jesus name.

I declare that today my days of affliction have expired.
Every power fighting against my breakthrough is expired.
Every hidden and dark prophesy against my destiny, expires today.
Every trained demon and Goliath spirit trying
to block my promotion is cast out.

Every Goliath speaking against my opportunities, and
that is seeking to see my demise is now cast out.
Goliath of failure, hindering spirit, spirit of delay, and
agents of the occult chanting against my name for evil or
failure. In the name of Jesus, your work is canceled.
God of Elijah, cut the power of darkness off my things. Arise now!

To every Goliath giant I declare that today your time is over.
I speak into my bedroom that every Goliath spirit
against marriage dies. And I call forth fruitfulness,
peace, and unity to dwell in marriage.

Every Goliath spirit in my living room. I break your
power now in the name of Jesus. Only the presence
and the glory of God will dwell in my living room.

Every Goliath spirit, lingering in my kitchen.
I command you to release your hold and leave now,
I cancel your power in the name of Jesus,
and the Blood of the Lamb.
Only the name of Jesus is welcome in my kitchen.

I command the Goliath spirit in my bathroom that has set
up its bed to be now removed and cast into the abyss.

Spirit of the living God arise in my home
and set up permanent residence.
Witchcraft spirit, I come against you in Jesus
name. Financial burdens are now canceled.

Lord, release wealth in my home.
Release breakthrough.
Release prosperity. Now!

I declare that every power of darkness must go.
And the power of the Lord Jesus Christ has
been lifted as a bloodstone banner today.
I am free from the power of the Goliath spirit, in the name of Jesus.
Amen and amen.

....

Prayer of Declaration

Jesus, today I declare that I recover my broken destiny.

....

DAY 4

John 15: [7] *If ye abide in me, and my words abide in you, ye shall ask what ye will, and it shall be done unto you.*

BREAKING GENERATIONAL CURSES

Every power that is blocking my progress,
I command you to stop now.
Be removed from my substance.
Every satanic attack interfering with my prosperity is canceled.
Every charm, spell, and witchcraft working
against my life is broken now.
Your time is up. You are paralyzed, your schemes are blocked.

Every hindering spirit that is blocking open
doors is cast into the burning abyss.
Territorial spirits that are attacking my financial
release, I command you to get out of my finances.
Every evil power speaking out against my blessings,
I silence you by the power of Jesus' name.

Every serpent that is lingering or moving over my finances, I
curse it according to the authority given to me in God's Word.
All power has been given to me over the schemes of the enemy.
Every dark chain and demonic agent against my promises,
I break it now by the power of the name of Jesus.
Kindred spirits that attacked my offspring, I cut
you off from my DNA––I detach myself from you,
and previous generational curses now!
And declare that they are uprooted and burned
by the power of the Holy Spirit.

Every demonic attack that comes against my wealth,
I send you back with the finger of God.
Every power assigned to stop my wealth, lose your hold and go.
Let the favor of God locate me now.
A financial release appears, now. Send prosperity now.
Lord Jesus, according to the Word - Your
blessings shall overtake me.
So, I ask you to send Your overtaking
prosperity, wealth and favor now.
I receive it now, by faith in Your finished work.

Let the glory of God shine forth now, upon my finances.
Enough is enough. I possess everything that belongs to me.
TODAY! I call for supernatural RELEASE,
In Jesus name,
Amen and Amen.

....

Prayer of Declaration

Jesus today I declare that I am free from every generational curse over my life.

....

Part-II
Activate Your Blessings

Thou shalt also decree a thing, and it shall be established unto thee: and the light shall shine upon thy ways.

-----Job 22:28

Chapter 2
Prayers That Introduce the Blessings of God

DAY 5

Deuteronomy 28:2-6² And all these blessings shall come on thee, and overtake thee, if thou shalt hearken unto the voice of the Lord thy God.³ Blessed shalt thou be in the city, and blessed shalt thou be in the field.⁴ Blessed shall be the fruit of thy body, and the fruit of thy ground, and the fruit of thy cattle, the increase of thy kine, and the flocks of thy sheep.⁵ Blessed shall be thy basket and thy store.⁶ Blessed shalt thou be when thou comest in, and blessed shalt thou be when thou goest out.

INVOKING BLESSINGS

Lord Jesus, I come to you today,
To break off the spirit of destitution and lack.
I reject every spirit of financial debt,
And paralyze the backbone of poverty.
Anyone, or anything withholding my prosperity, I
command it to expire in the name of Jesus.

I curse and disarm financial slavery that are
hindering my financial breakthrough.
I call forth the Abrahamic blessing to be visible in my life.
Starting today, I declare that my status will change from
having thousands in my account to becoming a millionaire.

Lord Jesus, let my request bring forth angelic assistance.
I ask YOU to send ministering angels to release
Your blessings upon my finances.
I walk in divine health and wealth under
an open heaven of favor.
I declare that doors and opportunities are opening for me.
Lord Jesus, I thank you for taking me from lack to abundance.
I seal this prayer in the mighty name of Jesus.
Amen and amen.

....

Prayer of Declaration

Jesus today I declare all the blessings of this prayers over my life.

....

DAY 6

Proverbs 10:^{22} The blessing of the Lord, it maketh rich, and he addeth no sorrow with it.

THE BLESSINGS OF ABRAHAM

Lord Jesus, according to Your Word,
I exercise the authority You give me to destroy the works of the devil.
I break every chain of poverty and destroy the spirit of lack.
Let the God of Abraham grant me the wealth that belongs to me.
Lord Jesus, as Abraham was very rich in cattle, silver, and gold.
Give me access to that same blessing that Abraham had.
Multiply my possession until it overflows.
Remember me, O Lord and allow me to walk
in favor both with you and man.
Command YOUR blessing upon my life
And let the world see and call me blessed.
From today, I declare that the blessings
will flow to my next generation.
I pray all these promises in Jesus' mighty name.
Amen and amen.

....

Prayer of Declaration
Jesus, today I declare the Abrahamic blessings over my life.

....

DAY 7

Deuteronomy 28:1-13 And it shall come to pass, if thou shalt hearken diligently unto the voice of the LORD thy God, to observe and to do all his commandments which I command thee this day, that the LORD thy God will set thee on high above all nations of the earth:² And all these blessings shall come on thee, and overtake thee, if thou shalt hearken unto the voice of the LORD thy God.³ Blessed shalt thou be in the city, and blessed shalt thou be in the field.⁴ Blessed shall be the fruit of thy body, and the fruit of thy ground, and the fruit of thy cattle, the increase of thy kine, and the flocks of thy sheep.⁵ Blessed shall be thy basket and thy store.⁶ Blessed shalt thou be when thou comest in, and blessed shalt thou be when thou goest out.⁷ The LORD shall cause thine enemies that rise up against thee to be smitten before thy face: they shall come out against thee one way, and flee before thee seven ways.⁸ The LORD shall command the blessing upon thee in thy storehouses, and in all that thou settest thine hand unto; and he shall bless thee in the land which the LORD thy God giveth thee.⁹ The LORD shall establish thee an holy people unto himself, as he hath sworn unto thee, if thou shalt keep the commandments of the LORD thy God, and walk in his ways.¹⁰ And all people of the earth shall see that thou art called by the name of the LORD; and they shall be afraid of thee.¹¹ And the LORD shall make thee plenteous in goods, in the fruit of thy body, and in the fruit of thy cattle, and in the fruit of thy ground, in the land which the LORD sware unto thy fathers to give thee.¹² The LORD shall open unto thee his good treasure, the heaven to give the rain unto thy land in his season, and to bless all the work of thine hand: and thou shalt lend unto many nations, and thou shalt not borrow.¹³ And the LORD shall make thee the head, and not the tail; and thou shalt be above only, and thou shalt not be beneath; if that thou hearken unto the commandments of the LORD *thy God, which I command thee this day, to observe and to do them:*

END TIME BLESSINGS

In the name of Jesus,
I deploy the key of financial restraint to
gain access to long-lasting wealth,
Blessing, abundance, and prosperity.
From the throne room perspective, and the heaven of heavens,
By the superior power of the Blood of Jesus.

I command the Midianite curse,
The curse of vain labor, foolish errands,
The curse that swallows down wealth to be revoked,
In the name of Jesus.

I command the spirit of self-sabotage,
And any personal weakness that the
enemy is using to get me to spoil
My blessings and financial breakthroughs.
Let that power and the access of the enemy be revoked,
Shut down and permanently destroyed,
In the name of Jesus.

I command the financial hijackers,
And every satanic diversion deployed against my finances,
To be arrested and blocked.
I destroy every satanic restriction and demonic embargo imposed

To enforce disappointment at the point of breakthrough,
In the name of Jesus.

I cast and tear down every stronghold and
satanic attack over my finances,
And I rebuke the spirit of the prince of Persia,
That is blocking the release of my finances.
I will prevail and be established,
In the oil of financial wealth and supernatural increase,
In the name of Jesus.

In this season, of God's financial release,
I command the blessings of God to overtake
me, according to God's Word.
I command the blessing to overtake me, so, that,
I shall walk in my blessing,
I shall receive my blessing,
I shall be a blessing,
I shall be the head and not the tail,
I shall be the lender and not the borrower
In the name of Jesus.

I call forth God's angel of divine release
To deliver, my blessing,
My abundance,
My wealth and prosperity in this season,
That God has assigned to release my financial increase,
In the name of Jesus.

Lord Jesus according to Your promises,
I stand in position and wait for you to COMMAND,
My end time blessing of wealth and prosperity
That belongs to me,
In this season of release.
I seal this prayer with your divine Blood,
And in the powerful and mighty name of Jesus,
Amen and amen

....

Prayer of Declaration
Jesus today I declare the end time blessing over my life.

....

DAY 8

3-John 1:² Beloved, I wish above all things that thou mayest prosper and be in health, even as thy soul prospereth.

DESTROYING POVERTY AND CALLING FORTH PROSPERITY

Today I declare that the altar of poverty of my place of
birth, working against my prosperity, be burned to ashes.
Every stronghold of mental and spiritual poverty in
my life, be uprooted by the fire of the Holy Spirit.
Any covenant in my life that is strengthening
the stronghold of poverty be broken.

Every stronghold of poverty, in the place where I am living now, and in my place of work, or around any place that I am in contact with, is pulled down, in the name of Jesus Christ.

Today, I declare continuous prosperity upon my destiny.
O Lord create opportunities for my prosperity.
I bind, and cast out, every negative Word enforcing poverty in my life.
Every evil plot against my prosperity and wealth,
I destroy it by the power of the name of Jesus and the fire of the Holy Spirit, every weapon of poverty targeted against my life from birth and until now.

I command, in Jesus name, that every stronghold of poverty in my life be destroyed.
Every evil power retaining my prosperity, must release it to me now.
Every stigma of poverty in my life is stricken by the power of the Blood of Jesus.
Let every evil seed of generational poverty, from my mother and father side, dry up from its root.
I command the stronghold of inherited poverty in my life to be pulled down by the blood of Jesus.

Holy Spirit deliver me from the captivity of the spirit of poverty.
Every curse of poverty, placed upon my family, be consumed by the fire of the Holy Spirit.
Every curse of poverty, spoken into my life by household wickedness, witchcraft, necromancy, voodoo, witches, Obada, or Panduit worshiping, I cancel your power, blind your eyes, and cripple your movement. Go back to your sender.

Jesus, arise, and undo every trap of poverty in my life, and let me walk in the prosperity and wealth that You have for me since before the foundation of the world.
In the name of Jesus,
Amen and amen.

....

Prayer of Declaration
Jesus, today I cast poverty out of my life, and release the YOUR prosperity in my life.

....

Testimony

I received a testimony from an individual who, believed God for her student loan of over $200,000.00 to be paid-off, and it was canceled. She doesn't have to pay back any student loans. The loan was canceled after I prayed.

I was on my Thursday prayer line and prayed for financial release. Someone believed God and had high faith. The next day, she received a check for $10,000.00. I know that God supernaturally sent the money to her address.

....

Wealth––Health & Prosperity is yours. Declare your abundance now.

....

Part III
Prophetic Prayers

Calling a ravenous bird from the east, the man that executeth my counsel from a far country: yea, I have spoken it, I will also bring it to pass; I have purposed it, I will also do it.

-----Isaiah 46:11

"...and calleth those things which be not as though they were." -----Romans 4:17

Chapter 3
Prayers That Brings Wealth

DAY 9

Proverbs 10:²² The blessing of the Lord, it maketh rich, and he addeth no sorrow with it.

GOD'S INCREASE

Lord Jesus,
Let Your wealth increase flow in my life
Like Jabez prayed, I pray for a financial move to take place.
Enlarge my territory.
Enlarge my borders.
Increase my finances and wealth,
And point me away from the enemy.

I stand on Your Word;
Knowing that You are the God Who keeps His promises.
I believe in Your Word

I accept Your Word
And hide Your Word in my heart.

As of today,
Anything that is hindering my progress,
That is blocking my development,
And anything that is stopping my fulfillment,
I apply your blood on it. The Blood of Jesus.

I will forever keep Your Word on my lips,
My heart,
My soul,
My body,
And my mind.
Therefore, I take the keys of authority,
That You have given me to exercise the supernatural power,
In my life,
In this time,
And in this season.

So, as of today,
I will always be the head and not the tail.
I will be the lender and not the borrower.
I will be above and not beneath.
I will take control over my entire situation,
Over my troubles,
Over my pain,
And I rebuke the enemy in Jesus' name.

Eradicate, Satan's plot and plan over my finances
and command him to release my wealth, and the
prosperity in the threshold of my basket.
I seal this prayer, with your name,
The name that is above every name,
The name of Jesus,
Amen and amen.

....

Prayer of Declaration
Jesus today I declare an increase over my life.

....

DAY 10

1-Kings 4:1-7 Now there cried a certain woman of the wives of the sons of the prophets unto Elisha, saying, Thy servant my husband is dead; and thou knowest that thy servant did fear the Lord: and the creditor is come to take unto him my two sons to be bondmen.² And Elisha said unto her, What shall I do for thee? tell me, what hast thou in the house? And she said, Thine handmaid hath not anything in the house, save a pot of oil.³ Then he said, Go, borrow thee vessels abroad of all thy neighbours, even empty vessels; borrow not a few.⁴ And when thou art come in, thou shalt shut the door upon thee and upon thy sons, and shalt pour out into all those vessels, and thou shalt set aside that which is full.⁵ So she went from him, and shut the door upon her and upon her sons, who brought the vessels to her; and she poured out.⁶ And it came to pass, when the vessels were full, that she said unto her son, Bring me yet a vessel. And he said unto her, There is not a vessel more. And the oil stayed.[7] Then she came and told the man of God. And he said, Go, sell the oil, and pay thy debt, and live thou and thy children of the rest.

DEBT CANCELATION

Lord, today I bow my head in adoration to you,
As I dismantle every demonic assignment attached
to my increase and overflow—break it.
Mighty angels of God scatter every hindrance of delay.
Every power that is giving confidence to my
enemy, I declare it burned from the root.
Every power over my home breaks NOW!

Every power that caused my family to suffer, today is cut off.
Every Goliath that comes against my possessions is paralyzed now.
Every voice of darkness speaking against
my wealth; I silence you now,
in the name of Jesus.

I declare loud and clear to the atmosphere;
my dry season is over.
From today, I will see the flow of wealth,
The flow of blessings,
The flow of prosperity,
The flow of breakthrough,
Today is a new day, today is a new season.

The ministering angels of the Lord
assigned to my financial miracle,
Release my abundance and overflow, NOW.
I command my financial miracle to step
into my bank account now.
Supernatural release locates my bank account now.
I declare wealth and finances over my financial resources
To overtake me now, in the name of Jesus.

God of Abraham, Isaac, and Jacob, grant
me my inherited portion now.
God of Elijah, arise now and defeat every enemy,
That stands out to hinder my financial resources.

I hold up the blood stain banner of Jesus over my finances,
In my checking and saving account.
Blessings of the Lord overtake me NOW.
I prophesy a twenty-four-hour breakthrough upon my life.

I decree it to be so, in the mighty name of Jesus,
Amen and Amen.

....

Prayer of Declaration

Jesus today I declare that I am free from all financial debt and I call forth Your blessings over my life.

....

DAY 11

Deuteronomy 28:⁸ The Lord shall command the blessing upon thee in thy storehouses, and in all that thou *settest thine hand unto; and he shall bless thee in the land which the Lord* thy God giveth thee.

COMMAND THE NEW SEASON

Lord Jesus, I come to you today,
As I deploy the key of financial restraint, to
gain access to long-lasting wealth,
Blessings, abundance, and prosperity,
From the perspective of the throne and the heaven of heavens,
By the superior power of the Blood of Jesus.

I command the Midianite curse,
The curse of vain labor,
The curse of foolish errands,
The curse that swallows down wealth to be revoked,
In the name of Jesus.

I command the spirit of self-sabotage
and any personal weakness,
That the enemy is using to get me to spoil my miracle,
My blessings and financial breakthroughs to get out of my life,
And let the access of the enemy be shut
down and destroyed permanently,
In the name of Jesus.

I command financial hijackers
And every satanic diversion deployed against
my finances to be arrested and blocked
In the name of Jesus.
I destroy satanic restrictions and demonic embargoes imposed
To enforce disappointment at the point of breakthrough
In the name of Jesus.

I rebuke and tear down every stronghold
and satanic attack on my finances.
I rebuke the spirit of the prince of Persia that
is blocking the release of my finances.
I will prevail and be established,
In the anointing of financial wealth and supernatural increase,
In the name of Jesus.

In this season, of God's financial release,
I command the blessings of God to overtake
me according to His Word.
I command the blessing to overtake me so that,
I will walk in my blessing,
I will receive my blessing,
I will be a blessing,
I will be the head and not the tail,
I will be the lender and not the borrower,
In the name of Jesus.

I call forth God's angel of divine release
To deliver my blessing,

> My abundance,
> My wealth, and all financial increase,
> including the prosperity, in this season
> that God has assigned for release.
> I decree that I am blessed.
> I decree that I will walk in my overflow.
> I decree I'm blessed, to blessed others,
> In the name of Jesus,
> Amen and Amen.

....

Prayer of Declaration

Jesus, today I declare the new season of God's wealth over my life.

....

DAY 12

Joshua 14:12-14 [12] *Now therefore give me this mountain, whereof the Lord spake in that day; for thou heardest in that day how the Anakims were there, and that the cities were great and fenced: if so be the Lord will be with me, then I shall be able to drive them out, as the Lord said.* [13] *And Joshua blessed him, and gave unto Caleb the son of Jephunneh Hebron for an inheritance.* [14] *Hebron therefore became the inheritance of Caleb the son of Jephunneh the Kenezite unto this day, because that he wholly followed the Lord God of Israel.*

GIVE ME, MY INHERITANCE

I come today by the power of the name of Jesus,
I bind every power against my breakthrough and prosperity.
Lord Jesus allow my finances to increase,
enlarge and promote itself.
Let my finances be protected by You so, that the enemy
will not be able to touch, smell or even see them.

Allow your power to protect my money––so, that
the spirit of debt and financial blockage will
be crippled, paralyzed and impotent.
I cancel, in the name of Jesus, every financial hindrance
against my wealth and block the spirit of lack over my money.

Every demonic seer hindering my prosperity is dismantled now.
Let the Spirit of God arise over my resources.
I call all financial agents of God to sit-on,
around, above and beneath my money.

Spirit of the living God surround my financial bank and allow
my money to bring increase, enlargement and double resources.
Every enemy of my breakthrough must go.
Satan, I command you to get off my stuff.
Get off my wealth.
Get off my prosperity.
Lose your hold and flee now.

> I command you to let go everything that you
> are hindering–in the Jesus' name.
> I receive everything that is mine according to God's promise,
> Now by the mighty name of Jesus.
> Amen and amen.

....

Prayer of Declaration
Jesus, today I declare YOUR inheritance over my life.

....

<u>Testimony</u>

I prayed for a woman who son was arrested because he was in the wrong company. I fervently prayed, and the next day he was released. All records dropped. Most amazingly, her son got a job three days after he was released.

One of our monthly financial partners lost her job for six weeks. She has been working on this job for ten years and feared that she would lose everything that she earned in this job. After I prayed, she received a phone call stating that she should return to work.

Every door this woman went through was closed. She became frustrated and angry at God because she couldn't pay her bills. I went in a time of prayers, and two days later she received a check for $6,000.00, from a company that she worked for over ten years prior. Wow, what payers can do.

For five years a woman had applied for disability and got no response. Family members have helped her and were tired of doing so. But the Lord directed me to pray specifically for her needs, and gave her a prophetic word that God, will release all the money that belongs to her in seven days. On the seventh day, she received a letter from the Social Security Administration stating that she will receive a check of over $60,000.00.

....

You are in your appointed season!
Declare your healing today.

....

Chapter 4
I Am Healed

DAY 13

Jeremiah 1:¹² Then said the Lord unto me, Thou hast well seen: for I will hasten my word to perform it.

Matthew 7:7-8 ⁷ Ask, and it shall be given you; seek, and ye shall find; knock, and it shall be opened unto you: ⁸ For every one that asketh receiveth; and he that seeketh findeth; and to him that knocketh it shall be opened.

GOD'S COMPLETE FULFILLMENT

Today I stand on the Word of God,
And the authority that God has given me in the Scriptures.
Therefore, I use God's Word to bring manifestation in my life.
According to God's Word and the power of my tongue:
I call forth every promise of God to come into my life.

Today I call forth everything that God has for me.
I call forth my healing, NOW—IN JESUS NAME.
I call forth deliverance for my family, NOW—IN JESUS NAME
I call forth wealth in my life, NOW—IN JESUS NAME.
I call forth financial breakthrough, NOW—IN JESUS NAME.
I call forth restoration in my life, NOW—IN JESUS NAME.
I call forth miracles in my life, NOW—IN JESUS NAME.
I call forth God's abundant harvest in my
life, NOW—IN JESUS NAME.

Every achievement that belongs to me,
I command it to locate me now.
I command love in my life,
Let your glory be seen through me.
Let your anointing be visible in my life,
Let your humility be present in my life,
As I dwell in Your secret place.
For Yours is the kingdom and the power, and the glory, forever.
In the name of Jesus,
Amen and amen.

....

Prayer of Declaration

Jesus, today I declare YOU are the fulfillment of God's Word over my life.

....

DAY 14

Isaiah 53:⁵ But he was wounded for our transgressions, he was bruised for our iniquities: the chastisement of our peace was upon him; and with his stripes we are healed.

James 5:13-15 ¹³ Is any among you afflicted? let him pray. Is any merry? let him sing psalms.¹⁴ Is any sick among you? let him call for the elders of the church; and let them pray over him, anointing him with oil in the name of the Lord:¹⁵ And the prayer of faith shall save the sick, and the Lord shall raise him up; and if he have committed sins, they shall be forgiven him.

PRAYERS OF HEALING

Today I stand in the authority of God's Word,
So I break the power of the enemy and walk in
God's authority to bring forth my healing.
I put all sickness under subjection,
And release God's signs and wonders.

I declare healing in my home by the power of Jesus Christ,
Healing over my life
Healing in my marriage
Healing in my body
Healing from diabetes
Healing from cancer
Healing from heart disease
Healing from AIDS

Healing from anxiety
Healing from depression
Healing from Arthritis
Healing from Asthma
Healing from dementia
Healing from Alzheimer
Healing from mental disorders
Healing from digestive disease
Healing from allergies
Healing from migraine headaches
By His stripes every sickness and diseases are healed.

I break every sickness, from its root and curse
it, with the name and Blood of Jesus.
Satan take your hands off my body,
And go back into the abyss, now.
I command God's healing, by the power and
the Blood of Jesus and His stripes.
I am healed, in the name of Jesus.

....

Prayer of Declaration

Jesus, today I declare YOUR healing over my life.

....

DAY 15

2-Timothy 1: ⁷ For God hath not given us the spirit of fear; but of power, and of love, and of a sound mind.

SOUND MIND

In the mighty name of Jesus,
I pray that every spirit of destruction working in
the mind, is subdued in the name of Jesus.
Today I command Satan and his demons to
come out of the mind of my loved ones.
Every spirit of the strong man, I command you to, get out, go!
Lose your hold off my loved ones. I break every
mental curse of destruction today.

Lord Jesus, just like YOU delivered the man
that was possessed by a legion of demons,
Heal the mind of *(Call out the person's name)*.
Deliver _____ *(Call out the person's name)*, from the
spirit of schizophrenia, paranoia, hallucination, depression,
anxiety, fear, delusion, confusion or schizoaffective disorder.
Give them a spirit of self-control, and of a sound mind.

Today I decree and declare that the power of the
Holy Spirit will grant complete healing, deliverance,
and miracle from every mental disease.
Bring balance to the life of my loved ones and
cause them to function as healthy individuals.

Thank you for deliverance from the spirit of the dark world and ushering (*call the name of the person*), into your marvelous light.
It's not by might nor by power, but by YOUR Spirit.
My spirit has been set free from the power
of slavery of the dark world
For he/she who the Son sets free, is free indeed.

Jesus, Your deliverance has been made known because
of the power of Your name and your blood.
You are a refuge for the oppressed; therefore,
I bring into captivity every thought
To the obedience of God's Word and the name of Jesus.
I declare that today God's healing results in a sound
mind, body, soul, and spirit in my loved one.
I seal this prayer in the name that is above all names,
In Jesus' mighty name,
Amen and Amen.

....

Prayer of Declaration

Jesus today I declare a sound mind over my family's life and myself as well.

....

DAY 16

Psalms 23:1-6 The LORD is my shepherd; I shall not want.[2] *He maketh me to lie down in green pastures: he leadeth me beside the still waters.³ He restoreth my soul: he leadeth me in the paths of righteousness for his name's sake.⁴ Yea, though I walk through the valley of the shadow of death, I will fear no evil: for thou art with me; thy rod and thy staff they comfort me.⁵ Thou preparest a table before me in the presence of mine enemies: thou anointest my head with oil; my cup runneth over.⁶ Surely goodness and mercy shall follow me all the days of my life: and I will dwell in the house of the* LORD *for ever.*

DELIVERANCE

Lord Jesus,
I come to you today, and I ask you to cleanse me,
and forgive me of all my sins, that may have
resulted in curses against me.
With the fruit of my lips and from the depths
of my soul, I ask for YOUR forgiveness.
Allow me to enter your throne room of mercy
to walk in YOUR deliverance.
I go behind the scenes to eradicate and remove every
Pharaoh spirit that may have taken hold of my life.

I break every spoken curse and spell that may
have been declared over my life, and any curses
resulting in disobedience, failure, financial debt,
miscarriage, second marriage, and unproductivity.
And I release growth, productivity,
happiness peace and joy in my life.

Lord Jesus,
I take the authority that you have given me
and ask You to anoint me now.
As I command every demonic spirit and break
its curse and hold off my family.
I break off every shackle, chain, habits,
Or any spirits that have tried to destroy my life.
I command my family to be set free.
I command my life to be free from every attack of
the enemy that hinders progress in my life.
I break every demonic assignment over my family.
Satan, I command you to release them right now!
From today onward, I will be free from every
spirit that is trying to hold me down,
And I commit myself entirely to the Lord, Jesus Christ.
I will now walk in the Spirit of Jesus so that I
can fulfill all the things of the Spirit.
For who the Son sets free, is free indeed.
I declare that I am free,
I am blessed and highly favor,
I am prosperous, and more than a conqueror.
Lord, I pray that You stand in agreement
with me, in Jesus' mighty name
Amen and Amen.

....

Prayer of Declaration

Jesus, today I declare that I am delivered in every area of my life.

....

DAY 17

2-Corinthians 12: ⁹ And he said unto me, My grace is sufficient for thee: for my strength is made perfect in weakness. Most gladly therefore will I rather glory in my infirmities, that the power of Christ may rest upon me.

STRENGTH

Lord Jesus, I thank you because you strengthen my heart,
You are my strength, and all my help comes from You.
My energy is down,
My motivation is gone,
But I know that with You at my side, I will arise.
I surrender every area of my will, mind, and emotions to You.
Let Your power rest on my weakness today.

I declare that I will receive power in my weakness,
I will walk in the strength of God's Spirit, and not
in the strength that the world has to offer.
Allow your strength to abide with me as I soar like an eagle,
Give me the power to run and not get warry, that I may
obtain the reward that you have, and awaits me.

Renew my strength that I may mount up with wings like eagles.
Lord help me lift my burdens, troubles and struggles to You,
So that I may be able to have success today.
You are my strength.
You are my source of grace.

You are the only one that can fix my brokenness and loneliness.

Lord Jesus, I am complete in you.

Thank you for the strength You give me every

second, minute and hour of the day.

For this, I will continue to rejoice and dwell in Your presence.

In Jesus name, I pray,

Amen and amen.

....

Prayer of Declaration

Jesus, today I declare that I recover the destiny that has been broken over my life.

....

Testimony

Demons would visit this woman's home every night. She could not sleep at night. She was restless, uneasy and very disturbed. One Thursday night I prayed on the prayer line and she began to walk all over her house. The following night she was able to sleep like a baby. Now her house is full of the presence of God.

For more than two weeks I've prayed for one of my monthly financial partner's mother to be healed from her sickness. She went to the doctor and took several tests, and the doctor reported that all her analysis was fine, and she was in the clear from the test and alignment of the health issues that she had. She does not need any surgery on her ovaries and she is cancer free. Isn't God a healer.

Someone accidentally found the program *"A Time Of Deliverance"* on the word network and began to listen weekly. One week while she was listening I instructed the viewers to write down the things you are believing God for. For over two years she had breast soreness. I did a general prayer for everyone and ask them to believe and have faith in God as I prayed. The next day she had no more soreness at all in her breast. Went to the doctor and was cleared of all sickness.

An individual has been following my television program on the Word Network for two months. She has been in bed with an incurable disease for more than nine months. She called the prayer line and I prayed for her and now she is off her bed of affliction and will be getting married soon.

....

Your words will form your world!
Declare Your opportunity today.

....

Chapter 5
Take Spiritual Authority

DAY 18

Job 38: ¹² Hast thou commanded the morning since thy days; and caused the dayspring to know his place;

COMMAND MY DAY

This is the day that the Lord has made;
Lord, let me rejoice in it now.
Today, I declare that my entire day will be prosperous,
I seek YOU this morning, like Abraham rose
early in the morning to seek Your face.
I arise to praise YOU.

Lord Jesus, I submit myself and entrust
my entire day into your hands.
I declare that YOU will have lordship over my day and
cause the enemy to be destroyed, and out of my way.

Let Satan's domain be overwhelmed by
the power of Your Holy Spirit.

I declare that today, I will walk in favor and
possess all that You have set aside for me,
In this day give me my portion.
Let me walk into new realms of authority.
I curse every power that will try to steal
my portion, let it be destroyed.

Let all Your blessings overtake me today,
Let all the promises that you have prepared
track me down and find me.
Let new dreams be birthed today.
Let new possibilities be manifested.
Let every breakthrough become a success.
I command the goodness of God to take place in my life today.

I declare that today a new season of my life begins.
A new season for my family, my ministry,
and opportunity in my workplace.
Changes are beginning to take place today in my community.
I command a new realm of influence this day.
I declare that today begins with a new and fresh anointing.
I put heaven in agreement with my assignment on the earth
and declare that today will be a day of possession.
I bind every power of darkness in the name of Jesus,
And decree that it will not interfere with this day.

Lord, I pray that YOUR ministering angels surround
my life and help me advance onward to my destiny.
Today I declare that I will have a victorious and prosperous day.
In the name of Jesus,
Amen and amen.

....

Prayer of Declaration
Jesus, today I declare that I recover the destiny that has been broken over my life.

....

DAY 18

Job 22:²⁸ Thou shalt also decree a thing, and it shall be established unto thee: and the light shall shine upon thy ways.

DECREEING GOD'S PROMISE OVER MY LIFE

Today I decree and declare the fulfillment
of God's Word in my life.
I decree and declare all of God's blessings for my life.
I decree and declare God's supernatural release in my life.
I decree and declare God's increase in my life.
I decree and declare more of God's power in my life.
I decree and declare God's overflow in my life.
I decree and declare God's divine favor in my life.

I decree and declare God's healing in my life.
I decree and declare God's miracle in my life.

I push myself into God's divine expectation, so that I may receive angelic visitation and God's divine transformation in my life.
I sprinkle God's supernatural abundance.
And declare God's favor and opportunity in my life, that I may see great and mighty manifestations of His Word in my life,
I seal this prayer in the name of Jesus,
Amen and amen.

....

Prayer of Declaration
Jesus today I declare all of YOUR written promises over my life.

....

DAY 20

Matthew 18:18-19 [18] *Verily I say unto you, Whatsoever ye shall bind on earth shall be bound in heaven: and whatsoever ye shall lose on earth shall be loosed in heaven.* [19] *Again I say unto you, That if two of you shall agree on earth as touching any thing that they shall ask, it shall be done for them of my Father which is in heaven.*

KEYS OF AUTHORITY

Lord Jesus,
Today I acknowledge that You have given me authority over the powers of darkness,

To tread on serpent and scorpions,
And over all the power of the enemy.

I decree that from now on,
I will use the power that you have given me.
I will use this power to destroy the works of Satan.
I will use the power you have given to me, to fight
against the struggles that come my way.
I will use the power of your name to override
every temptation and trial.

Lord Jesus,
Let me walk in YOUR supernatural authority,
Live by YOUR miraculous power,
Speak with the authority of your word,
And exercise all kingdom authority that
You have given me here on earth.

Therefore, from now on,
I will stand on Your Word,
And use Your Word when weapons are formed against me.
YOU have declared that the works that YOU have done,
I will also do in a greater way.

I am more than conquer,
I have the power of the Holy Spirit within me,
I have authority to bind and to release,
I have the keys to unlock and close every door,
And from now on I will use those keys.

Today I declare that I will walk fully in kingdom authority.
In the name of Jesus,
Amen.

....

Prayer of Declaration

Jesus, today I declare the authority of God over my life.

....

Never underestimate the power that is in the name of Jesus.
I declare that every attack of the enemy is dismantled!

Testimony

Demons were walking in this woman's house and tormenting her at night, and she couldn't sleep at night. I prayed the prayers to break demonic attacks, and the woman instructed me that something broke off from my home. Now her home feels very full of the presence of God and free. From all works of the enemy.

An individual that would join the prayer line every Thursday, would wake up in the mornings, and see white dust in front of her door and on her porch. She doesn't know who was doing it. It has been happening for three years, but when she came in contact with the ministry, things changed. I prayed a prayer, and something broke. The next day after I prayed, and she went in front of her home. There was no white dust. It's been three months now, and she have never seen any dust again on my porch.

During the time of prayer on the Prayer line, I began to pray and prophesied that someone would hear something by Friday, about an available apartment. The follow Thursday a woman received a call from the apartment management, that someone had just come in and informed them that they were moving out and immediately the apartment manager said that they thought about the person that I prophesied too and offered her the apartment, without any credit check.

....

Unlock heaven with your faith to obtain your breakthrough!
Declare your release today.

....

Chapter 6
Supernatural Breakthrough

DAY 21

JAMES 5:17-18[17] *Elias was a man subject to like passions as we are, and he prayed earnestly that it might not rain: and it rained not on the earth by the space of three years and six months.* [18] *And he prayed again, and the heaven gave rain, and the earth brought forth her fruit.*

James 5:17-18[17] *Elijah was a man with human frailties, just like all of us, but he prayed and received supernatural answers.*[aa] *He actually shut the heavens over the land so there would be no rain for three and a half years!* [18] *Then he prayed again, and the skies opened up over the land so that the rain came again and produced the harvest. (The Passion Translation)*

SUPERNATURAL RELEASE

Today I declare that every target of the enemy backfires. Every power that seeks to block or hinder my triumph, is defeated.

I paralyze the spirit of poverty.
I break every financial bondage.
Every power sitting on my wealth is cast out NOW!
I block every doorway and gateway of poverty over my life.
And open all the doors to prosperity.
Let the name of the enemy be annihilated
and let the power of Jesus stand.

KNOWER OF THOUGHTS delivers me.
Omnipotent and glorious One, grant me success.
Bestower of goodness, answer me now as I call on you.
I implore you to perform wonders for my loved
ones and myself, and when it is done,
Let it be known that it is Your miracle.
Begin your work today.

Lord Jesus, YOU have given me the power to get wealth—So,
let the power of wealth within me be released out in the open.
Reveal to me the keys to my prosperity.
Let the blessing of the Gentile be transferred into my account.
Let my life magnify You in every financial area.
Revive my blessing.
Return a double portion to my storehouse.

Lord, I implore you
Let my portion come from heaven.
Let my words and prayers find favor before You,
As I call forth finances to find me.
Enlarge my borders,

Let signs and wonders follow my finances.
I pray that the promised blessings made to Abraham,
Isaac, and Jacob, and their seed, be released on my life
in the name of Jesus. Bless my heritage forever.

Let the treasures of heaven send down rain in this
season to bless me from now until eternity.
Lord, let my prayers stand before you, day and night,
That you would provide for my every need
So that all nations of the earth will know
that you are the only true God.

Today, allow my supernatural release to be done on earth,
as heaven comes in agreement to bring my manifestation.
I declare supernatural miracles, healing, blessings, and
breakthroughs will happen within the next seventy-two hours.
I seal every spoken words of this prayer to show
evidence that the Lord watches over this prayer,
And hastens His Word to perform it.
In Jesus' mighty name,
Amen and Amen.

....

Prayer of Declaration
Jesus today I declare the supernatural release of God over my life.

....

DAY 22

Joshua 5:⁹ And the Lord said unto Joshua, This day have I <u>rolled</u> away the reproach of Egypt from off you. Wherefore the name of the place is called Gilgal unto this day.

FROM REPROACH TO OPPORTUNITY

Today I come in the mighty name of Jesus
And I command every reproach against my life and my family to be terminated by the power of the Holy Spirit.
I arrest all evil invaders assigned to infiltrate my success.
Every instrument that the enemy is using
to produce reproach in my life
Let it be destroyed in Jesus name.

Break the yoke of poverty that produces reproach over me.
Break the power of the enemy that causes stagnation in my life.
Break every hidden curses and reproach over my life.
Break every garment of reproach over my life.
Burn down the stronghold of reproach that hinders my life.
Every arrow of reproach towards my life, let it backfire now.
Lord Jesus expose every agent of witchcraft
that is trying to block my progress.
Every power of the enemy that is prolonging my troubles, distress, and financial delay, is defeated now in the name of Jesus.
I call Satan's plan frustrated.
By the power of the Blood of Jesus, all reproaches
against my life are dismantled––now.

I call forth my success––now.
I call forth open doors of favor––now.
I call forth open doors of opportunity––now.

Lord Jesus, allow your spoken words over my life to be manifested.
Let heaven and earth make a declaration
that it is written today––that the Blood of the
Lamb breaks all reproach over my life.

I seal this prayer in Your name,
The name that is above every name,
The name of Jesus,
Amen and Amen.

....

Prayer of Declaration

Jesus, today I declare the reproach is broken, and doors of opportunity swing open over my life.

....

DAY 23

Nahum 1:12-13 [12] Thus saith the LORD; Though they be quiet, and likewise many, yet thus shall they be cut down, when he shall pass through. Though I have afflicted thee, I will afflict thee no more.[13] For now, will I break his yoke from off thee, and will burst thy bonds in sunder.

SUPERNATURAL BREAKTHROUGH

Lord Jesus,
I come to YOU today,
As I lift my faith.
Build my trust and increase my confidence,
To receive Your supernatural breakthrough.
I break every demonic root.
I bind the strongman attached to the life of my resources.
Let the powers sponsoring evil decisions
against my breakthrough be destroyed,
And let the plan and purpose for
supernatural breakthrough prevail.
Let every spirit of Pharaoh drown in the Red Sea.
Let every evil imagination against me wither
from the source of my breakthrough.
And let every power eating up my spiritual path be destroyed,
And set the fire of the Holy Ghost to bring
forth my supernatural breakthrough.

Lord Jesus,
This week,
I expect a supernatural breakthrough from You,
Supernatural healing,
Supernatural deliverance,
Supernatural miracles,
And supernatural financial increase.
I will walk in the overflow of the supernatural.

I will walk in favor,
And I will walk in the abundance
That you have set aside for me
Therefore, I will remain focused to receive from You.

Today,
I command the heavens to lose every package that belongs to me.
I call forth a quick release.
I command the move of God upon my life,
Therefore, I patiently and faithfully await
To receive a shift from heaven to take place in my life.
Let Your will be done on earth this week.
Let the heavens send forth the overflow of
Your supernatural breakthrough,
Supernatural favor,
Supernatural abundance,
Supernatural healing,
Supernatural miracles,
And Your supernatural financial increase
That You have prepared for me.
I declare it to be so,
And seal this prayer, with the Blood and the
mighty name of our Lord Jesus Christ.
Amen and Amen.

....

Prayer of Declaration

Jesus today I declare a supernatural breakthrough over my life.

....

DAY 24

Matthew 6: [13] *And lead us not into temptation, but deliver us from evil: For thine is the kingdom, and the power, and the glory, for ever. Amen.*

MY RECOVERED DESTINY

Lord Jesus, I come to You today asking that You destroy,
Every device of witchcraft targeted to manipulate
my destiny; cut it off from my life.
I command the enemy of my financial
blockage to cease and desist its work.
I release myself from any inherited bondage.
I break off every evil force that is hindering my blessing.

Let the roots of family witchcraft be uprooted
from the foundation of my life.
Generational poverty, I pull you out from the root––NOW!
Every evil force that is consuming my
prosperity, I command it to stop.
Every strongman that is hindering my
finances, I revoke his authority.
I command every foundational strongman attached
to my life to be paralyzed in the name of Jesus.
Evil fingers, pointing towards my wealth, I stop you now.
I direct the finger of God to block and dismantle you.
Let all evil influences holding any of my
blessings in bondage, be released now.

Financial blockage hear the Word of the Lord now and stop.
I cut every demonic chain targeting my prosperity
and break it now in Jesus' name.

Spirit of the Living God take control of my wealth
and command it to be released NOW.
Father, I pray that You open the Heavens and release
over me your riches in glory by Christ Jesus.
I recover all that belongs to me.
Lord, I recover my destiny.
Restore me to the financial destiny that you have for me.
In Jesus name,
Amen and Amen.

....

Prayer of Declaration
Jesus today I declare that I have recovered all broken destiny over my life.

....

DAY 25

Colossians 4:³ Withal praying also for us, that God would open unto us a door of utterance, to speak the mystery of Christ, for which I am also in bonds:

OPEN PRISON DOORS

Lord Jesus today I come to YOU knowing
that you are the giver of all things.
I ask of you that you will cause all doors
to open for me in this season.
Every plan and effort that the enemy may try to use to block my
access to open doors, allow his effort to be destroyed today.
Every invisible target or sledge hammer that the
enemy may try to use against a door that is open to
me, I command his attack to stop in Jesus' name.

Lord, I declare that the enemy is defeated
and that all hindrances stop today.
Let every source blocking my breakthrough be undone.
Let every Satanic curse assigned to my
open door, be scattered to pieces.
Every altar bewitchment against my mother and father's
generations, I command you to cease and desist your work.
I send you back to the sender, backfire now, in the name Jesus.
Let God arise and uproot every stigma of Satan.
Every Satanic court pleading to stop my opportunity––I
curse you by the Blood of the Jesus.

To months and years of closed doors, I say: Open now!
In the name of Jesus, I destroy the works of
Satan geared to hinder and entrap my life.
As I walk through every door and
opportunity that God has for me,

> I speak it loud and clear to the atmosphere that
> all doors will be opened to me today.
> In Jesus name,
> Amen and Amen.

....

Prayer of Declaration
Jesus today I declare that I have recovered all broken destiny over my life.

....

<u>Testimony</u>

One Thursday night during our prayer line, I prayed and prophesied saying that money would begin to come in every week into someone's life. That was a Thursday night, the Saturday of that same week, a woman received a check of $5,456.00. The following week, she received $3,025.00. Three weeks after that, she received a check for $1,500.45. Money just keeps coming in the mail. she can't believe it. Is this real? She said! Every check she deposited was cleared. God supernaturally moved on her finances.

A widow's house was in foreclosure, and she needed $15,000.00 to keep her house. But I prayed for supernatural release, she believed it, and God did it for her. A job that she left more than seven years sent her a check. God smiled on her. She paid her mortgage and was able to keep her house.

"The money will be released to you in six days. All backed up rent for the past three months will be paid." Those were the words I prophesied and prayed over a woman's life. In six days, she received her three months, rent of $2,800.15. Prayers and the prophetic word did it.

....

Unlock heaven with your faith to obtain your breakthrough! Declare your release today.

....

Part IV
Walk In Your Freedom

If the Son therefore shall make you free, ye shall be free indeed.

-----John 8:36

Chapter 7
As for Me And My House

DAY 26

Joshua 24:[15] *And if it seem evil unto you to serve the Lord, choose you this day whom ye will serve; whether the gods which your fathers served that were on the other side of the flood, or the gods of the Amorites, in whose land ye dwell: but as for me and my house, we will serve the Lord.*

MY MARRIAGE IS HEALED

Lord Jesus
I lift my voice today and release Your power over my marriage.
Today I renounce any evil company that
will try to infiltrate our union,
I break it off and dismantle it now.
Every spirit that brings marriage destruction, I break it now.

I interrupt every spirit of bondage and
frustration over my marriage.

Lord, bridle my tongue from speaking any
harmful things against my spouse.
And any other tongue that rises against my
marriage, to bring destruction, confusion or
separation—I condemn it, by Your Blood.

Lord, let every evil hindrance that targets
my marriage, become unfruitful.
Every generational spirit that is trying to linger over my marriage,
Let it be dismantled today.

Curse every spirit of pornography, social media confusion,
sexual lust and internet distractions away from my marriage.
Destroy every thought of polygamy, threesome, foursome and
swinger spirits, that it may not come near my marriage.
Let all false prophecy against my marriage be silenced.
Every spirit that is challenging the progress, happiness, and
peace in my marriage, I command it to be broken off now.

I thank You for the spouse You have given me.
Teach us to depend continually in Your power,
in good and challenging times.
My marriage is honorable, and my bed is undefiled.
Let me and my spouse go higher spiritually each day with you.
Let me and my house serve you always.
I speak laughter, peace, joy, happiness, love
and togetherness over my marriage.
In Jesus name,
Amen and amen.

Prayer of Declaration

Jesus today I declare Your healing power upon my spouse and over my life.

DAY 27

Genesis 2: [18] *And the Lord God said, It is not good that the man should be alone; I will make him an help meet for him.*

SINGLE

Lord Jesus,
You created humankind as male and female.
I declare that every decision over my life, in
my singlehood will be prosperous,
I cover myself today with the Blood of Jesus.
I pray that You would help me to live a
godly life as a single Christian,
Protect my eyes from the spirit of lust today.
Allow me only to see the things that You want me to see,
Hear the things that You want me to hear,
And obtain only the things you desire that I obtain.
Allow my Boaz to find me like you caused Boaz to find Ruth.

Let me delight myself in your glory and walk in the
beauty of ashes, even when I feel discouraged.

Carry me in your bosom until I become the Esther of my time.
Keep me pure, holy and consecrated like Mary,
until my Joseph finds me for himself.
Lord fill my heart with the will to do Your
work and let my mind stay on you.

Magnify my anointing, so that it will attract
others to live a powerful single life.
Lord help me always to remember, that when trials
come, loneliness and distress comes, that You
will favor me and pour out Your love on me.

I declare that I am fearfully and wonderfully made
and that You have great plans for my life.
As You have decreed, no good thing will You withhold
from those that love the Lord. Release my good things.
I thank you, Lord,
In Jesus name.

....

Prayer of Declaration

Jesus today I declare that I have recovered all broken destiny over my life.

....

DAY 28

Genesis 2:22-24 [22] And the rib, which the Lord God had taken from man, made he a woman, and brought her unto the man. [23] And Adam said, This is now bone of my bones, and flesh of my flesh: she shall be called Woman, because she was taken out of Man. [24] Therefore shall a man leave his father and his mother, and shall cleave unto his wife: and they shall be one flesh.

PRAYING FOR A SPOUSE

Lord Jesus
I come boldly before your throne, to express the
desire of my heart for a loving and God-fearing
spouse with whom to spend the rest of my life.
I ask that you bring the right spouse to my life, that loves you first,
Grant me a spirit of patience to wait for the person You have for me.

I come to You in agreement with Your Word, and in Your name.
Knowing that it was You, who created
humankind, as male and female.
After Creation, You, established the family
with the union of a man and a woman.
You knew me before I was born and declared
that it is not good for a man to be alone.
You created Eve to be Adam's help mate.
So, today I pray that you will have my Adam find me.
You said that a man that findeth a wife, findeth a good thing.
Let my Adam find me (Or let Eve find her man).

Help me to make the right choices, as I prepare myself to
meet that person that you have already chosen for me.
I pray for my future spouse's mind.
Let today be the day, that I may encounter
the spouse you have for me.
I thank you in advance as I obtain my heart's desire today.
In Jesus name,
Amen and amen.

....

Prayer of Declaration
Jesus today I declare that I have recovered all broken destiny over my life.

....

DAY 29

1-Samuel 1:27-28 [27] For this child I prayed; and the Lord hath given me my petition which I asked of him: [28] Therefore also I have lent him to the Lord; as long as he liveth he shall be lent to the Lord. And he worshipped the Lord there.

PROTECT MY CHILD

Lord Jesus, I come to you today believing
that You are my shield and buckler.
I ask you today to protect my children,
Let them come to the knowledge of Your truth.

Continue to give them integrity in their heart,
that they may seek your face daily.
Increase their knowledge,
Increase their wisdom and cause them always to please you.
Lord Jesus, cause my child to be very compassionate towards
others and fill their hearts with peace, joy, and happiness.
Lord Jesus, you know the hearts of my children and today,
I implore you to give them the fullness of your
grace to the fulfillment of your promise.
Lord Jesus, if my child is out of connection with you,
Bring them back to the fold of your fellowship.
Bring them into unity with you, on a daily basis.
Guard their hearts against the attacks of Satan,
And protect their souls from being contaminated
with the cares of this world.
Let every creative ability of my child come forth.

Lord Jesus, just like Samuel was given back to You from Hannah
I dedicate my children to you, as they are covered
under the protection of Your Blood.
Please keep my children under your protection and
let Your Blood be on the doorpost of their heart.
I commit my child in Your presence, asking you to
keep them safe day and night, night and day.
I pray this in Your great and mighty name
In the name of Jesus,
Amen and Amen.

Prayer of Declaration

Jesus today I declare that I have recovered all broken destiny over my life.

DAY 30

Psalms 91:3-7 ³Surely he shall deliver thee from the snare of the fowler, and from the noisome pestilence. ⁴He shall cover thee with his feathers, and under his wings shalt thou trust: his truth shall be thy shield and buckler. ⁵Thou shalt not be afraid for the terror by night; nor for the arrow that flieth by day; ⁶Nor for the pestilence that walketh in darkness; nor for the destruction that wasteth at noonday. ⁷A thousand shall fall at thy side, and ten thousand at thy right hand; but it shall not come nigh thee.

HOUSE PROTECTION

Lord Jesus, today I come to your secret place,
And command all powers of the enemy to cease and desist.
Every spirit of darkness over my home, I
curse you in the name of Jesus.
Every evil force monitoring my surroundings,
stop now by the power of Jesus.
Every demon associated with the spirit of lack,
you have no control over my home.

Evil spells that bring torment against my sleep at night
crumple to the ground now by the power of Jesus' name.
Every demon attacking my dreams is now
sent back to burn in the abyss.
Every evil spirit that disturbs my dreams at home,
I rebuke you by the power of Jesus' name.

All sexual demons in my dreams that cause
torment must go back to their sender.
Every strongman that is attacking my family
blessings, happiness, and progress, I lose the
power of the Holy Spirit upon you now.

Witches, wizard, warlocks and voodoo spirits, I cancel
your attack over my home now, in the name of Jesus.
I change your plan and purpose over my
life and cripple your actions now.
Only the Lord Jesus is welcome in my home. All other
forces directed by the enemy leave my house.
I declare that only the presence of the
Lord will dwell in my home.

From now on, no explicit music, ungodly movies,
or foul words will be spoken in my home, but only
words that bring forth the glory of God.
Today, I declare that every Goliath is fallen and has been
defeated, and the name of the Lord is lifted in my home,
In Jesus name,
Amen and amen.

....

Prayer of Declaration

Jesus, today I declare that I have recovered all broken destiny over my life.

....

DAY 31

2-Timothy 1: ⁶ *Wherefore I put thee in remembrance that thou stir up the gift of God, which is in thee by the putting on of my hands.*

3-John 1: ² *Beloved, I wish above all things that thou mayest prosper and be in health, even as thy soul prospereth.*

PRAYING FOR MY CAREER AND SPIRITUAL GIFTS

Almighty God and Savior,
I come to You today, believing that You
are the giver of every good gift.
For many are called but few are chosen, and
I thank you today for choosing me.
No good thing will you withhold to them that walk uprightly.
You have given us the power to get wealth,
for every area of our life.
Wealth in my finances
My ministry
My job,
My career

And my family.
Let Your emboldening power cause my
success and breathe upon my destiny.

Lord Jesus, today I pray that You give me the mantle of Elijah.
Cause every arrow pointing against my destiny be destroyed.
Every Satanic weapon formed against my calling, my
gifting, and my career, be rendered ineffective.
I refuse to retire before my appointed time. So, keep my
mind, spirit, and body, secure in the power of Your blood.
Only allow Your glory to be the shadow of my destiny.
Let your strength and power lead me
on the ladder of my success.
You have made me the head, and not the tail so, allow
me to tarry in the tower of authority, each day of my
life and put me in place to embellish Your power,
So that I may inherit all that You have set aside for
me at the work of my ministry and my calling.
I declare fulfillment over my life and open doors during
this century into which You have birthed me.
Thank you for every opportunity of working in Your vineyard.
And allowing me to shine forth.
Let my gift be stirred up in every season of my
life, where I will always bring forth fruit.
Thank you, Lord,
In Jesus name,
Amen and Amen.

Prayer of Declaration

Jesus today I declare that I have recovered all broken destiny over my life.

Additional Prayer!

Jeremiah 1: [5] Before I formed thee in the belly I knew thee; and before thou camest forth out of the womb I sanctified thee, and I ordained thee a prophet unto the nations.

OPEN MY WOMB

Spirit of the living God fall afresh on me.
Let the power of your Holy Spirit open my womb,
So that I may conceive without miscarriage.
Let there be no stillbirth nor any spirit of abortion.
Every negative report that was given to me about
sterility is now banned from my vocabulary.
Let the spirit of failure and demonic inquires, lose its hold now.
Every spirit targeting my loss and un-fruitfulness,
Let it be immediately destroyed.

Lord Jesus, secure my womb,
And set your hand upon the incubator of my uterus,
so that the embryo of my unborn child can make its
appearance in the delivery place on the ninth month.

Lord Jesus, I've been redeemed from the curse of the law;
Therefore, I expect to produce my bundle of joy.

Like you opened Hannah's womb, open mine.
Let me laugh like Sarah did, at the appointed time of conception.
Drive me to the place of childbearing, so,
I can hear the words "Mommy."
Undo every curse that tries to approach
my birth canal and placenta.
Let not my child bearing pain multiply.
Allow me to experience no child bearing pain.

I decree within nine months that the labor
room will see the blossom of my fruits
Let me bring forth the child with the
correct gender of my choice.

Today I implore the power of YOUR fertilization,
So, I wait with expectation to become pregnant.
I thank You for the gift of life.
It is by Your power that I will be able to give birth.
I seal this prayer, in the mighty name of Jesus,
Amen and Amen.

....

Prayer of Declaration
Jesus today I declare that my womb is open and the fruit of childbearing over my life.

....

I Prayed, and God Answered!

Dear Lord, thank you for answering the prayers of your people. Thank you for the manifestation, deliverance, healing, breakthrough, supernatural release, and blessings upon your people. All these are done in Jesus name, Amen.

Then you will call on Me and you will come and pray to Me, and I will hear [your voice] *and* I will listen to you. -----**Jeremiah 29:12 (Amplified Bible)**

CPSIA information can be obtained
at www.ICGtesting.com
Printed in the USA
BVHW041424300422
635483BV00002B/472